MARGO GURYAN

Lead Sheets: Words/Music/Chords

Cover design by Coral Amende

ISBN 978-1-4234-9979-4

A PUBLICATION OF
DARTMOOR MUSIC

DISTRIBUTED BY

HAL•LEONARD®
CORPORATION
7777 W. BLUEMOUND RD. P.O. BOX 13819 MILWAUKEE, WI 53213

Contents

CAN YOU TELL

Margo Guryan

CALIFORNIA SHAKE

WORDS AND MUSIC BY
RICHARD BENNETT
MARGO GURYAN

UN-DER-GROUND IT STARTS TO RE-AR- RANGE. ____
LIV-ING THROUGH A MI-CRO-SCOP-IC DEATH. ____

YOU'D BET-TER GET UP __ AND RUN FOR A DOOR-WAY. __
YOU'D BET-TER HOLD ON. __ THE WORST IS-N'T O- VER. __

(INSTRUMENTAL)

NO TIME FOR THINK-ING. YOUR LIFE IS AT STAKE.

EV-'RY-ONE'S DO-ING THE CAL-I-FOR-NIA SHAKE. __

CAL-I-FOR-NIA SHAKE. __

COME TO ME SLOWLY

Margo Guryan

DON'T GO AWAY

Margo Guryan

The 8:17 Northbound Success Merry-Go-Round

Margo Guryan

GOOD-BYE, JULY

WORDS & MUSIC BY
MARGO GURYAN

Hold Me Dancin'

WORDS AND MUSIC BY
MARGO GURYAN

(REPEAT 'TIL FADE)

The Hum

WORDS and MUSIC by:
MARGO GURYAN

THE HEAT IS DOWN AND THE LIGHTS ARE LOW, THE EAST IS BUR-IED IN AN I- CY SNOW. THE WEST IS FOL-LOW-ING CRI-SIS RULES— THEY CAN'T GO SWIM-MING IN THEIR SWIM-MING POOLS— AND THE TAPES GO HM——— HM——— HM——— THE PRI-CES RISE AND THE MAR-KET FALLS, THE TRUCKS GO SLOW AND THE CON-GRESS STALLS THE V. P. LEFT WITH THE DOUGH HE TOOK AND THE

I DON'T INTEND TO SPEND CHRISTMAS WITHOUT YOU

Words and Music by
MARGO GURYAN

I Love

Margo Guryan

I THINK A LOT ABOUT YOU

WORDS & MUSIC BY
MARGO GURYAN

AND___ ___WHAT I DO --- I THINK A LOT A - BOUT___

YOU. ___ ___

YOU. ___ ___

I'D LIKE TO SEE THE BAD GUYS WIN

WORDS & MUSIC BY
MARGO GURYAN

IT'S ALRIGHT NOW

WORDS & MUSIC BY
MARGO GURYAN

LOVE

Words & Music by
Margo Guryan

WHEN DO YOU GET _____ TO BE _____ SOME-ONE _____ WHO _____ CAN

AD- GIVE _____ AND LIVE WITH-OUT HURT-ING _____ SOME-ONE

YOU LOVE

WHY DO WE GROW _____ AND NEV- ER SHOW _____ THE LIT-TLE THAT WE

KNOW OF LOVE

LOVE SONGS

Words and Music by
MARGO GURYAN

MOST OF MY LIFE

Shine

MUSIC AND LYRIC BY
MARGO GURYAN

YOU MAKE ME SHINE SHINE SHINE SHINE____

LOOK-ING AT ME WITH STARS IN YOUR EYES

TRY-ING TO SAY WHAT I'VE AL-WAYS WANT-ED TO

KNOW YOU WANT ME TO KNOW THAT YOU'RE

MINE MINE MY IT FEELS GOOD TO BE-

LIEVE IN SOME-ONE IT'S BEEN A LONG TIME A LONE-LY TIME IT'S BEEN A

HARD TIME AN EMP-TY TIME SINCE AN-Y-ONE CAUSED ME TO
MADE ME TO FEEL

SHINE SHINE SHINE SHINE SHINE
FINE FINE FINE FINE FINE

This song can be played note for note against Bach's "Jesu, Joy of Man's Desiring."

Someone I Know

Margo Guryan

Please Believe Me
(A Watergate Love Story)

WORDS and Music by:
MARGO GURYAN

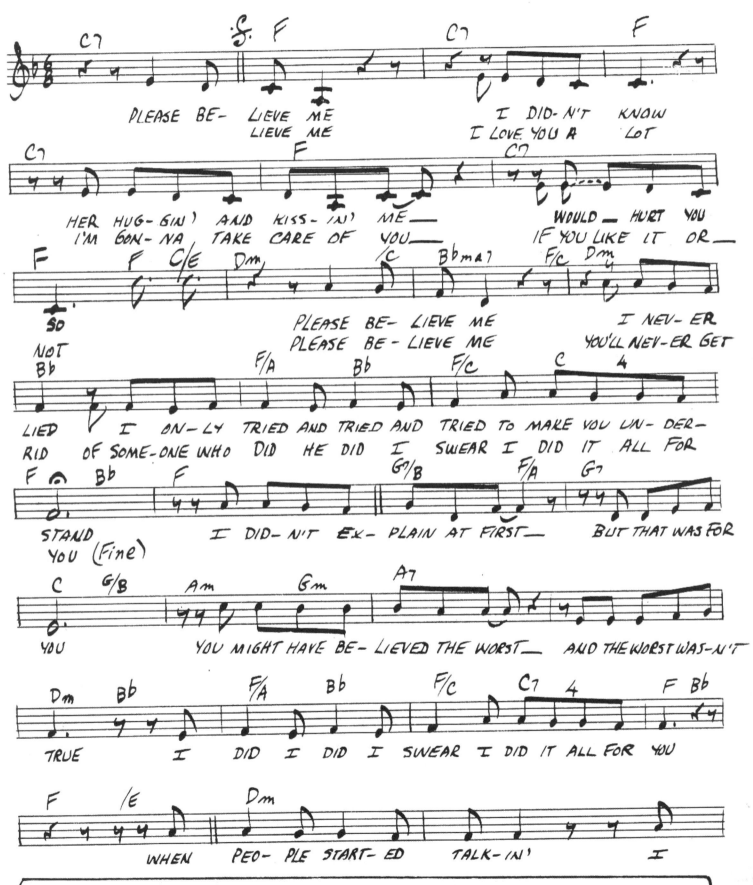

36

PROOF IN BLACK AND WHITE BUT THERE ARE-N'T AN-Y LET-TERS COU-SIN
WAT- ER GATE HO - TEL __ IF SUE AND I HAD BEEN THERE IT WAS

SUE CAN'T E- VEN WRITE IT WAS VI-CIOUS IN-NU-EN- DO THAT CON-
WRONG FOR THEM TO TELL __ I KNOW YOU'LL UN-DER-STAND IT WHEN THE

VINCED YOU I HAD SINNED BUT I'D NEV- ER LEAVE YOU TWIST-ING SLOW-LY
FACTS ARE YOURS TO SEE __ I SWEAR I NEV- ER TOUCHED HER SHE WAS

SLOW - LY IN __ THE WIND PLEASE BE-
MAK- ING LOVE__ TO ME PLEASE BE-

SOMETHING'S WRONG WITH THE MORNING

Margo Guryan

What Can I Give You

MUSIC AND LYRIC BY
MARGO GURYAN

WHAT CAN I GIVE YOU, WHAT WOULD MAKE YOU HAP-PY?

WHAT CAN I DO,— WHAT CAN I SAY TO MAKE THE BAD TIMES GO A-WAY? IT'S BEEN A

LONG, LONG TIME SINCE I'VE SEEN YOU SMILE, AND I'VE BEEN

WANT-ING TO DO SOME-THING A-BOUT IT FOR A LONG, REAL LONG WHILE.

WHAT CAN I GIVE— YOU TO DRIVE A-WAY THE SAD-NESS?

WHAT CAN I BUY, WHAT CAN I TRY, TELL ME WHAT I CAN DO?— IT'S BEEN A

LONG, LONG TIME, AND YOU KNOW I KNEW YOU WHEN YOU USED TO BE HAP-PY;—

WHAT CAN I GIVE YOU TO MAKE YOU HAP-PY A - GAIN?—

SUN

WORDS AND MUSIC BY
MARGO GURYAN

Sunday Morning

WORDS AND MUSIC BY
MARGO GURYAN

TAKE A PICTURE

Words and Music by
MARGO GURYAN

Think Of Rain

WORDS AND MUSIC BY
MARGO GURYAN

THOUGHTS

Words and Music by
MARGO GURYAN

F
A7
Dm
F7
Com - ing home,
Feel - ing new,
Bb
A7+6
A7
Dm
Dm/C
Climb the stair,
O - pen the door,
G/B
Bb Maj. 7
Dm/A
G
You're not there
an - y - more,
Gm7
C7
Am7
Dm7
Emp - ty room,
Lots of tears,
Gm
C7
F sus 4
F
Bb
(No - bod-y hears)
Call your name.... No one hears me,
No one

TIMOTHY GONE

WORDS & MUSIC BY:
MARGO GURYAN

Values

WORDS and MUSIC by:
MARGO GURYAN

YOURS ARE NICE, THEY FIT YOU LIKE A GLOVE YOU'VE SEWN ___
YOURS ARE GOOD, THEY'VE SEEN YOU THROUGH THE

TOO BAD I'VE GOT TO FIND MY OWN.

BAD TIMES YOU'VE KNOWN SOR-RY I'VE

GOT TO FIND MY OWN.

I DON'T KNOW HOW MAN-Y TIMES I'VE RE- LIED ON YOU TO
I KNOW YOU'VE THOUGHT A-BOUT ME WHEN YOU WANT-ED TO

SEE ME THROUGH ___ NEV-ER AN O-RI- GIN-AL THOUGHT IN MY HEAD ___
AF-TER YOU ___ MAY-BE THATS THE WAY ___ YOU BE-LIEVE ___ PEO-PLE ARE ___

I THINK I'M START-ING TO THINK THERE WAS
I MUST BE CRA-ZY TO LOOK FOR AN

"YES I AM"

Words & Music
MARGO GURYAN